AMERICA'S MOST WINNING TEAMS™

MICHIGAN FOOTBALL

MARTIN GITLIN

rosen publishing's
rosen central

New York

Published in 2014 by The Rosen Publishing Group, Inc.
29 East 21st Street, New York, NY 10010

Library of Congress Cataloging-in-Publication Data

Gitlin, Marty.
Michigan football/Martin Gitlin.—First edition.
    pages cm.—(America's most winning teams)
Includes bibliographical references and index.
ISBN 978-1-4488-9397-3 (library binding)—
ISBN 978-1-4488-9423-9 (pbk.)—
ISBN 978-1-4488-9426-0 (6-pack)
1. Michigan Wolverines (Football team)—History—Juvenile literature.
2. University of Michigan—Football—History—Juvenile literature. I. Title.
GV958.U52863G58 2014
796.332'630977435—dc23

2012045525

Manufactured in the United States of America

CPSIA Compliance Information: Batch #S13YA: For further information, contact Rosen Publishing, New York, New York, at 1-800-237-9932.

CONTENTS

INTRODUCTION

The greatness of a college football team is not measured solely by win totals. It is not determined only by championships won. It is not evaluated simply by the number of all-Americans that have graced its uniform. It is not judged merely by the passion of its fans. The finest programs in America boast all of those features. One could argue that the University of Michigan is perched atop that list.

The Wolverines entered the 2013 season leading the nation with 904 victories all-time. They have captured eleven national titles. They have won forty-two Big Ten crowns, more than any other team, including archrival Ohio State. They have placed thirty-four players and coaches into the College Football Hall of Fame.

And their fans? Their average attendance of 112,179 in 2011 set an all-time National Collegiate Athletic Association (NCAA) record, and in 2012 they beat their own average attendance record with 112,252 fans, according to ESPN.com. Michigan Stadium has been nicknamed "The Big House" for its huge seating capacity and sellout crowds.

The history of Michigan football has been marked by consistent success for more than a century. The Wolverines wasted no time emerging as a force in college football.

A crowd of 110,343 packs the Big House on September 17, 2011, to watch the Wolverines dismantle in-state rival Eastern Michigan, 31–3.

One reason for their immediate achievement on the field was continuity in coaching. Michigan was unlike other programs, which changed coaches frequently around the turn of the twentieth century. Legendary coach Fielding Yost established the most powerful team in the country upon his arrival and maintained greatness for nearly three decades.

Nearly every coach that followed well into the 2000s was given time to create his own winning environment. The result was success in recruiting the finest players throughout the nation. For more than one hundred years, some of the greatest talent in the history of the sport passed through Ann Arbor on the way to stardom in the National Football League (NFL).

CHAPTER 1

"FIELDING" A GREAT TEAM

Michigan football was born on a scorching hot afternoon in Chicago, Illinois, on May 30, 1879. As if to proclaim themselves a national power from the very beginning, the Wolverines dominated their rivals from nearby Racine College.

Play was rough, especially for a Racine player named A. C. Torbert. A *Chicago Tribune* article the following day told the story: "No bones were broken, but Torbert was stretched out on the turf," it read. "A bucket of water however revived him."

The Wolverines broke no bones that day, but they broke the spirit of many a foe in their early years. They played just ten games between 1884 and 1887, but they won them all. During the last three years of that period, they outscored their opponents, 222–0. They had begun to forge an era of dominance that lasted until the Great Depression gripped the country in 1933.

The program had yet to establish the continuity in coaching that would distinguish itself in later years. But it did not matter before the turn of the twentieth century. Every coach won. During one five-year stretch beginning in 1894, Michigan earned a record of 39-7 with three different coaches. The 1898 team finished 10-0 and posted six shutouts.

Fielding Yost coached the most dominant college football teams in the country during the earliest years of the twentieth century. His Wolverines were known for their explosive offense and stifling defense.

FINALLY FINDING A FULL-TIME COACH

The Wolverines had captains, but no coaches from 1879 to 1890. Seven coaches came and went over the next ten years. In 1901, however, the school attracted a dedicated, competitive thirty-year-old coach named Fielding Yost. He immediately formed what many still believe is the finest team in college football history.

The Michigan teams of the early 1900s did not merely win. They were virtually perfect in performance. They lost just one game during their first five years under Yost, during which time they outscored their opponents by a combined score of 2,821–42.

Yost earned the nickname "Hurry Up" for the way his offenses scored points so quickly. His defenses were equally powerful. The 1901 team did not surrender a point.

Perhaps his most satisfying triumph came that year in the first-ever Rose Bowl Game in Pasadena, California, played against Stanford, the team he had coached

THE STORY OF WILLIE HESTON

The Michigan teams of the early 1900s were nicknamed "Point-a-Minute" for their ability to score quickly. Nobody was scoring them faster than halfback Willie Heston.

Heston came all the way from San Jose State in California to join the Wolverines in 1901. He had played the year before against Stanford, whose coach Fielding Yost was about to take the same job at Michigan. His talent caught the eye of Yost, who convinced him to join the Wolverines and study law.

It worked out perfectly. Heston starred on four Michigan teams that compiled a combined record of 43-0-1. He was 5 feet 8 inches (1.7 meters) tall and weighed 190 pounds (86 kilograms), but he could run the 100-yard dash in ten seconds. His speed devastated defenses. He was a mere freshman when he exploded for 170 yards rushing against Stanford in the Rose Bowl on New Year's Day 1902. He went on to score seventy-one touchdowns in his four years with the Wolverines.

His law studies also proved beneficial. Heston became a successful attorney in Detroit. But he never forgot the importance of staying in shape. He continued to run a half mile (805 m) every morning until the age of seventy-five.

the previous season. The Wolverines emerged from that showdown with a 49–0 victory. The game was never even completed. The Cardinals were so thoroughly beaten that they walked off the field in the third quarter and never returned! The game was so lopsided that another Rose Bowl was not played for another fourteen years.

One of the villains of the day for Stanford was Michigan fullback Neil Snow, a baseball and track standout who finished his college career in a blaze of glory. He rushed for 107 yards and scored five touchdowns in the win.

Yost and the Wolverines were just warming up. They continued to dominate the Western Conference. They won game after game by ridiculous scores. Their 130–0 dismantling of West Virginia in 1904 remains the largest margin of victory in Division I college football history.

NEW CHALLENGES

Michigan left what became known as the Big 9 Conference in 1907, opting for an independent schedule. The Wolverines

The 1904 national champion Michigan Wolverines were arguably the greatest college football team ever assembled. They outscored their opponents by a combined total of 567–22 in winning every game.

Star halfback John Maulbetsch, who starred for Michigan from 1914 to 1916, was known as "the Michigan Cannonball" for his powerful style of running with the football.

soon slipped from unbeatable to merely great. The level of competition was improving. Opposing defenses learned to slow down the high-powered offense. No Yost team from 1907 to 1917 won every game, but the Wolverines still recorded a 66-18-7 mark during that period. The end of that stretch and beyond was highlighted by individual and team greatness.

The first in a long line of premier offensive players was all-American halfback John Maulbetsch, whose relentless style of running earned him the nickname "the Michigan Cannonball."

Future College Football Hall of Fame center Ernie Vick arrived the year after Maulbetsch left. But the finest Wolverines of that era shared the same first name. Quarterback Bennie Friedman and end Bennie Oosterbaan powered Michigan teams that from 1923 to 1927 compiled a record of 34-6.

Friedman helped revolutionize the sport by bringing the forward pass to Michigan. His tosses were things of beauty and easy for receivers to catch, according to noted *New York*

Daily News sportswriter Paul Gallico. "When a Friedman pass reaches the receiver it has gone its route," Gallico wrote. "The ball is practically dead. The receiver has merely to reach up and take hold of it like picking a grapefruit off a tree. That is Benny's secret, and that is why so many of his passes are completed. He is the greatest forward passer in the history of the game."

ANOTHER GREAT BENNIE

Oosterbaan was among the finest all-around athletes in the history of college sports. He excelled in baseball and basketball. But he was certainly ready when the football season rolled around. He earned all-American honors every year from 1925 to 1927. He led the conference in scoring with eight touchdowns in 1925. He returned a recovered fumble 60 yards for a touchdown to give the Wolverines a victory over Minnesota.

The Yost era ended as it began—with perhaps the most dominant program in the country. His 1925 team did lose one game, but it won its seven others by shutout and captured the Big Ten championship. His 1926 Wolverines tied for the title. When he retired after that season, it was feared that the greatness of Michigan football would leave with him. As it turned out, there was nothing to worry about.

CHAPTER 2

CONTINUING TO ROLL

Fielding Yost had a dream. He envisioned the Wolverines performing in the largest football stadium in America. He yearned to see 120,000 fans cheering their team to victory. So when he became athletic director in 1921, he was driven to make his dream a reality.

The university administration worked to stop him. Yost battled construction problems. He overcame troubles financing the project. Nothing stopped him.

The venue turned out to be a bit smaller than Yost imagined, but it was still the biggest college-owned stadium in the nation. It seated 84,401 fans when it officially opened for the third home game of the 1927 season. The Wolverines rose to the occasion as the deafening sellout crowd spurred them on to a 21–0 victory over Ohio State. Their performance on the field the next six years proved worthy of their new home.

That is, thanks to Coach Harry Kipke. The former Wolverines star halfback and punter took the coaching reins in 1929 and transformed the team into a national champion in 1932 and 1933. His Wolverines lost just one game from 1930 to 1933.

Kipke built a tremendous offensive line behind premier quarterback Harry Newman. The group was anchored by all-American center Charles Bernard and

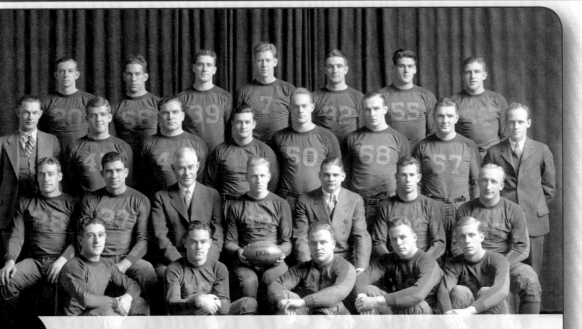

The undefeated 1930 Michigan team was coached by Harry Kipke *(second row, third from right)*, starred quarterback Harry Newman *(front row, far left)*, and halfback Willie Heston *(front row, second from right)*.

tackle Frances Sistert, a future College Football Hall of Famer. Michigan also relied on a stifling defense that yielded just 81 points in thirty-one games during those four seasons.

Just as quickly as the Wolverines rose to greatness, they collapsed. They followed their second straight national title year by losing seven of eight games in 1934 and sinking to last place in the Big Ten.

A demoralizing incident set the tone for disaster. Michigan was scheduled to host Georgia Tech in the third game of that season. But the southern school refused to show up unless Kipke benched star wide receiver Willis Ward, the first black Wolverines player in forty years. Rumors circulated that Georgia Tech players would seek to injure Ward.

Tom Harmon was one of the finest all-around players in the history of the college game. He excelled on offense, defense, and even special teams.

Many Michigan students protested. About 1,500 of them signed a petition demanding that Ward be allowed to play. Demonstrations were held on campus. Yet when the game began, Ward was not in uniform. He was humiliated. Many of his angry teammates threatened to quit. Among them was center Gerald Ford, who later served as president of the United States.

The Wolverines won, but that proved to be their only victory of the season. They stumbled to the worst period in team history. They sported a 10-22 record from 1934 to 1937. They were disgraced by archrival Ohio State during that time, losing all four games by a combined score of 114–0.

NEW COACH, SAME RESULTS

The lopsided defeats to the Buckeyes played a huge role in Kipke being fired and replaced by Fritz Crisler. Kipke did do one thing right off the field while his Wolverines struggled on the field. He recruited a running back named Tom Harmon.

TOM TERRIFIC

Michigan star halfback Tom Harmon had become a household name by his junior year. His photo was splashed on the cover of *Time* magazine in 1939. The article called him "a gregarious, lantern-jawed six-footer with a Tarzan physique" who runs "with the power of a wild buffalo and the cunning of a hounded fox."

In his first game as a senior, against the University of California, he returned the opening kickoff 94 yards for a touchdown. He followed that with an 86-yard scoring run on his first carry. He later scored touchdowns of 70 and 65 yards. One California fan grew so frustrated that he jumped onto the field and tried to tackle Harmon himself. He, too, failed.

Harmon later emerged as a hero as a fighter pilot in World War II, earning a Silver Star and Purple Heart after escaping near-death in battle. His injuries robbed him of his speed and power, cutting short his career with the NFL's Los Angeles Rams.

He was undaunted. He fulfilled his dream of becoming a sportscaster. He wed model Elyse Knox and fathered Mark Harmon, who later starred as a quarterback for the UCLA Bruins and became a successful television actor.

Arguably the greatest player in Michigan history, Harmon immediately transformed the team back into a winner.

Harmon rushed for 2,134 yards, scored 33 touchdowns, and even threw 16 touchdown passes during his three seasons at Michigan. He led the nation in scoring in 1939 and 1940, when he earned the coveted Heisman Trophy.

He capped his brilliant career in 1940 by single-handedly destroying Ohio State. He rushed for 139 yards, completed ten of 11 passes for 151 yards and 2 touchdowns,

Michigan player Ryan Van Bergen proudly hoists the Little Brown Jug, given annually to the team that wins the game between Michigan and Minnesota. The Wolverines had just clobbered the Golden Gophers, 58–0, in 2011.

intercepted 3 passes, and ran one of them back for a touchdown. He even averaged 50 yards a punt in the 40–0 triumph. It remains one of the greatest all-around performances in college football history.

Yet Michigan could not reach its goal of a national championship or Big Ten title with Harmon gracing its uniform. Its nemesis was Minnesota, which beat the Wolverings in each of the years from 1938 to 1940. Michigan lost four games between those years. Three of them were to the Golden Gophers.

The Wolverines continued to win in the early 1940s despite the loss of many players to World War II (1939–1945). Crisler changed college football forever in 1945 by introducing the two-platoon system, a system where two separate units of players were used for defense and offense. Crisler kept them fresh and allowed them to display their best attributes by using them only on offense or defense.

He also proved to be quite the innovator in calling plays. He utilized a wide variety of plays and formations. But the unbeaten season required to win a national championship continued to elude him. His teams lost at least one game in his first nine seasons.

CROWN FOR THE WOLVERINES

Then came 1947. The Wolverines swept through the regular season undefeated that year behind elusive fullback Jack Weisenberger and a defense led by future NFL star Len Ford that recorded four shutouts. They forged a Rose Bowl showdown with the University of Southern California (USC). The Trojans were no pushovers. Their only loss was to Notre Dame, the top-ranked team in the country.

Wolverines halfback Bob Chappuis turns the corner for a long gain in the 49–0 triumph over Southern California in the 1948 Rose Bowl.

They were no match for Michigan. Weisenberger scored three touchdowns, and all-American quarterback Bob Chappuis threw for two more in the 49–0 victory. It was the same score as when Michigan defeated Stanford in the 1902 Rose Bowl.

The Wolverines boasted talent all over the field. Legendary sportswriter Red Smith believed them to be by far the best team in college football after witnessing the lopsided defeat of USC. His words were recounted in the book *Game Day: Michigan Football*: "Michigan showed such a superlative poise and versatility in every department, such a wealth of offensive weapons and the talent to use them that it seemed a sacrilege to mention any other college team in the same breath."

The Wolverines, however, were mentioned in the same breath as Notre Dame. Associated Press declared the Fighting Irish national champions. The last chance for Crisler to win the crown was gone. He stepped down after that season and was replaced by Bennie Oosterbaan, another Michigan legend. Oosterbaan took the baton from Kipke and ran with it in 1948. This time, the Wolverines were not to be denied their ultimate goal.

CHAPTER 3

OOSTERBAAN OUSTED, BUMPED BY BUMP

The Wolverines were expected to collapse in 1948. Fritz Crisler was no longer their coach. Replacement Bennie Oosterbaan was starting over. Star halfback Jack Weisenberger was gone. So was quarterback Bob Chappuis.

They had ended the previous season on a fourteen-game winning streak. Most believed that would end quickly. A national championship? Forget it.

The 1948 Wolverines featured no player that ran for more than 330 yards. Quarterback Chuck Ortmann completed fewer than half his passes. Their three most utilized rushers averaged a meager 3.1 yards per carry. Their only great player was tackle Alvin Wistert. They did not scare their opponents.

All they did was win. They won with long touchdown passes and a defense that yielded just 4.9 points a game to rank best in the country. They were 3-0 with two straight shutouts heading into their showdown against unbeaten Northwestern. Michigan entered the game ranked fourth in the nation and looking up one spot at the Wildcats. After dominating Northwestern, 28–0, the Wolverines catapulted to number one. They would remain there almost the rest of the year.

They put an exclamation point on their 1948 season with a 13–3 victory over archrival Ohio State. The rules

STORY OF THE WOLVERINES

The nickname for Michigan sports teams traces back to the early 1860s. Theories abound as to its origin. The wolverine is a ferocious animal and the largest in the weasel family. But there is debate as to whether it even existed in the state at that time. Some believe wolverine pelts were swapped by fur traders within its borders in the 1800s.

Another theory revolves around one of the most famous military leaders in American history. General George Armstrong Custer is best known for his reckless attack against the Sioux and other

Star player Bennie Oosterbaan and new mascot Biff the Wolverine were honored along with the dedication of Michigan Stadium when it opened in 1927.

Native American peoples that resulted in his death at the Battle of the Little Bighorn in 1876. But more than a decade earlier, he led a Michigan cavalry brigade of the Union army during the Civil War. His Michigan soldiers fought so bravely and fiercely that Custer named them "Wolverines." The Wolverines defended the Union line at the critical Battle of Gettysburg and played a key role in surrounding the army of Confederate general Robert E. Lee at Appomattox Court House, where Lee surrendered to Union general Ulysses S. Grant and ended the Civil War. According to that theory, Michigan then became known as the Wolverine State and the University of Michigan followed suit by giving its sports teams the same nickname.

at that time prevented teams from participating in the Rose Bowl in consecutive years. But the Wolverines had nothing left to prove. They were declared national champions for the first time since 1933.

Oosterbaan was named national Coach of the Year by his peers. *New York World-Telegram* writer Lawrence Robinson expressed his view that it was the right choice. "[The coaches] knew what Oosterbaan must have faced, taking over a championship team, generally rated No. 1 in the country in 1947 ... and that it had lost its entire backfield, both tackles, the center and the star end," he wrote. "They realize what it took to rebuild a team and keep it at a winning tempo. . . . They also knew that in all football there is no more solid citizen than quiet, modest Bennie Oosterbaan."

GOOD, BUT NOT GREAT

Quiet, modest Bennie Oosterbaan could not maintain that level of excellence. His teams remained strong and won

Big Ten titles the next two years, but they lost at least two games every season from 1949 to 1958.

His last hurrah was 1950. The eyes of the college football world were on the annual Michigan–Ohio State showdown on Thanksgiving weekend that year. The conference championship was on the line. The Buckeyes had been the top-ranked team in the nation just a week earlier.

The city of Columbus, Ohio, was hit with a massive snowstorm. The temperature dropped to 10° Fahrenheit (-12° Celsius), while 30-mile-per-hour (48-km/hr) freezing winds howled through the stadium. Though eighty-five thousand Ohio State fans bought tickets, only the heartiest souls showed up.

The 1950 "Snow Bowl" showdown in Columbus between Ohio State and Michigan proved to be one of the most memorable games in the storied rivalry. The Wolverines overcame the weather and the Buckeyes for the victory.

The players could barely see on the field through the whiteout conditions. Fearful of losing yards trying to move the ball on offense, the teams often did not bother waiting four downs to punt. Ortmann, who served as the Michigan punter, even booted the ball on first down.

The Wolverines scored the winning touchdown with forty-seven seconds left in the first half when linebacker Tony Momsen blocked a punt and fell on it in the end zone. The 9–3 victory gave them their fourth consecutive Big Ten crown and propelled them into the Rose Bowl in 1951 against California.

They took the momentum from the "Snow Bowl" win and ran with it. The Wolverines upset the fifth-ranked Golden Bears, 14–6, on two fourth-quarter touchdowns by fullback Don Dufek and Chuck Ortmann's fifteen of nineteen pass completions.

The victories over Ohio State and California saved an average season and ushered in a long period of mediocrity. The only all-American produced during the next thirteen years was Ron Kramer, who starred as an offensive and defensive end in the mid-1950s before helping the Green Bay Packers to multiple NFL titles.

CHANGE AT THE TOP

Oosterbaan continued to sport winning records, but the losses sprinkled in angered Michigan fans who had grown accustomed to rooting for championship teams. His Wolverines collapsed to a 2-6-1 record in 1958, after which he resigned. His departure brought memories of a prediction he made that was published in a *Time* magazine article on November 24, 1958, after he had coached Michigan to a national title. "I'm on top now, and there is a lot of backslapping," he had said. "But what

Quarterback Bob Timberlake runs for a gain in the 1965 Rose Bowl victory over Oregon State. The win marked a highlight during a period of struggles for the Wolverines.

of seasons to come? Let me lose the opener, or a couple of other games next fall, and then watch how I'm blasted."

Replacement Bump Elliott would soon learn the truth to those words. He had been revered as a Michigan halfback in the late 1940s. But he was greatly criticized as a coach. His Wolverines sunk to a record of 20-23-2 in his first five years at the helm. Most frustrating was that they lost every showdown but one to archrival Ohio State during that time.

The light in a long period of darkness for the Michigan football program shined through in 1964 behind quarterback Bob Timberlake, running back Mel Anthony, and defensive back Rick Volk. They set the tone for a fine season when they upset a great Navy team. They ended a four-game losing streak to the Buckeyes with a 10–0 victory that propelled them into the Rose Bowl.

Oregon State was no match for a Wolverines team that had soared to number four in the country. The game featured an 84-yard touchdown run by Anthony that was exceeded only by the jaunt of a little pig! A pig made its way onto the field at the end of the first half and scampered 100 yards from one end zone to the other. The feat prompted a rousing ovation from the 100,423 fans.

The Anthony scoring run was the longest in Rose Bowl history. It is no wonder he was named Most Valuable Player in the 34–7 victory.

The 1964 Wolverines were merely a one-year wonder for Elliott. His teams reverted to being unexceptional. By the end of the decade, it was clear the program needed to go in a new direction. A young, charismatic coach was about to lead Michigan football into another era of greatness.

CHAPTER 4

UPSET OF THE CENTURY

The Wolverines were rolling in 1968. They were enjoying their finest season since 1964. They boasted explosive offensive talents such as end Jim Mandich and running back Ron Johnson, who followed the blocks of tackle Dan Dierdorf. All were ticketed for NFL stardom.

The showdown against unbeaten Ohio State promised to be an epic battle. But that promise was not realized. The Buckeyes scored 29 points in the second half and rolled to a 50–14 victory. Never mind that Ohio State was on its way to the national championship and is still considered perhaps the finest college football team ever. The Wolverines were humiliated. The lopsided defeat motivated coach Bump Elliott to resign.

It was believed that to beat Buckeyes coach Woody Hayes, the new coach would have to understand him. The result was the hiring of Miami of Ohio coach Bo Schembechler, who played under Hayes and served as his top assistant at Ohio State.

Schembechler ruled with an iron fist. He made certain his players and coaches were motivated by the winning tradition of Michigan football. His practices were more exhausting than any of his players had ever experienced. Many players hated Schembechler. Some even quit the

Legendary Michigan coach Bo Schembechler, who turned his team into a consistent winner, is shown here reacting to a play in the 1990 Rose Bowl against the Southern California Trojans.

team. But the ones that remained were in better shape than anyone wearing a different uniform.

The greatest coaching rivalry in Big Ten history and arguably in all of American sports was about to begin. It started on the fall afternoon of November 22, 1969. The Wolverines entered on a four-game winning streak. But the Buckeyes had destroyed all their opponents. Michigan was regarded as just another victim on their path to a second straight national crown.

Tackle Jim Brandstatter recalled his feelings heading into that game in a book titled *What It Means to Be a Wolverine*. A sophomore at the time, he wanted to win for the older players who had experienced the lopsided defeat to the Buckeyes the year before. "Everyone in the world cringed at the thought of playing Ohio State in 1969," he wrote. "They were the best thing since sliced bread. But we knew we could beat them. Bring on the Buckeyes!"

THE SHOWDOWN BEGINS

The Buckeyes rolled downfield for the first touchdown of the game. But when Michigan halfback Billy Taylor sprinted 28 yards for a score to give his team a 14–12 lead, the crowd of 103,588 at Michigan Stadium sensed an upset. They grew more confident when Wolverines defensive back Barry Pierson set up another touchdown with a 60-yard interception return.

In the second half, the defense blanked a Buckeyes team averaging 46 points a game. It was over. The scoreboard told the tale: Michigan 24, Ohio State 12. The Wolverines had achieved one of the greatest upsets in the history of American sports—at least to everyone but

Three Southern California tacklers converge on Michigan ball carrier Don Moorhead during the 1970 Rose Bowl, won by the Trojans. The Wolverines struggled to win bowl games under Coach Bo Schembechler.

themselves. The humdrum reaction of Schembechler was expressed by author George Cantor in his book, *Michigan Football: Yesterday and Today.* "We knew we were going to win from the very beginning," Schembechler crowed.

Michigan lost to USC 10–3 in the Rose Bowl in 1970, but it did not seem to matter. The players were more concerned about Schembechler, who suffered a heart attack the night before.

He recovered nicely. He was healthy enough to recruit the greatest players in the country. His teams in the early 1970s were among the best in all of college football.

THE TIE THAT CHANGED COLLEGE FOOTBALL

Frustration was the prevailing emotion for the Wolverines in the early 1970s. They forged a 30-2-1 record from 1972 to 1974 and embarked on a twenty-one-game unbeaten streak, their longest in twenty-five years. Yet they never played in a bowl game.

Why? Because both losses and the tie came against Ohio State. Big Ten teams were not allowed to play in any postseason game but the Rose Bowl. The Wolverines were left out in the cold.

The Wolverines sprinted to a 9-0 record in 1973 before a 10–10 tie against the unbeaten top-ranked Buckeyes. It was assumed league officials would vote to allow Michigan to play in the Rose Bowl because the Buckeyes had participated the previous year. Ohio State coach Woody Hayes even wished the Wolverines good luck in California.

The Big Ten voters decided the Buckeyes had a better chance to win and selected them instead. Michigan coach Bo Schembechler was furious. He nearly cried when he informed his players. Michigan fans threatened a lawsuit.

The reaction forced the Big Ten to allow non-champions to play in other bowl games. The Wolverines took advantage in 1975, but lost to the Oklahoma Sooners in the Orange Bowl in January 1976, by a score of 14–6.

BOWL GAME BLUES

There was just one big problem. The loss to the Trojans began a disturbing trend. Schembechler's teams could not win a bowl game until 1981. The Wolverines lost their first five Rose Bowl games under Schembechler and their first seven bowl games overall. Their defeat to Stanford in the 1972 Rose Bowl ruined their undefeated season and shot at an undisputed national championship.

The program was also stifled by the rule that no team could participate in the Rose Bowl in successive years. Michigan won or tied for four straight conference crowns starting in 1971, but played in just one bowl game during that stretch.

The rule was soon rescinded, but the Wolverines lost Rose Bowl games in 1976, 1977, and 1978 after beating Ohio State in each of those years. The rivalry with the Buckeyes lost some of its luster when Hayes was fired following the 1978 season. Schembechler earned a 5-4-1 record in his personal battles against Hayes in what became known as "the Ten-Year War."

ESPN.com columnist Pat Forde believed the Ohio State–Michigan rivalry has never been more compelling than when

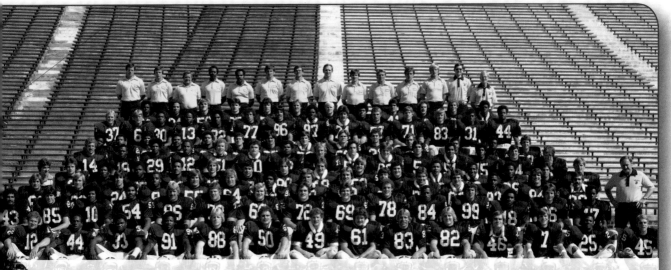

The 1977 Wolverines, shown here, soared to number one in the national rankings before a mid-season loss to Minnesota sent them reeling. They remained unbeaten throughout the rest of the regular season.

it featured Schembechler versus Hayes. "Those games embodied everything that makes the sport so compelling: sky-high stakes, immense pride, intense competition, unwavering will, extreme physical and mental toughness, great athleticism, healthy respect for the opposition and a reverence for tradition," Forde wrote.

Schembechler won no consensus national championships during his twenty-one years as coach, but he had no losing seasons. He returned the program to elite status. The Wolverines won or shared eight Big Ten titles from 1970 to 1978 while forging a record of 96-15-3.

He also produced at least one first-team all-American in every year but three from 1969 to 1982. Included were future NFL stars such as Mandich, Dierdorf, guard Reggie McKenzie, defensive back Dave Brown, and wide receiver Anthony Carter. Safety Thom Darden and quarterback Jim Harbaugh also emerged as NFL standouts.

Schembechler finished his career with just two Rose Bowl triumphs. Some Michigan fans did not believe their team could have a successful season without winning a national championship. They would be forced to wait nearly a decade for that dream to become a reality.

CHAPTER 5

CARR DRIVES WOLVERINES TO A TITLE

B o Schembechler suffered a heart attack as he prepared his team for the Rose Bowl in December 1969. He must have experienced a feeling of déjà vu that same month in 1987. He was not on the sideline when Michigan played Alabama for the first time in the Hall of Fame Bowl. He was recovering from quadruple bypass surgery. His time as coach of the Wolverines was nearing the end. He yearned to go out on top.

Mission accomplished. Schembechler's teams won successive outright Big Ten titles in 1988 and 1989 for the first time since 1947 and 1948. He then handed the reins to Assistant Coach Gary Moeller.

Schembechler had recruited some of the finest offensive talent in team history, including prolific quarterback Elvis Grbac. But wide receiver Desmond Howard provided the most excitement.

Howard delivered one exciting moment after another during his senior season in 1991. The first occurred with Michigan beating Notre Dame, 17–14, in week two. The Wolverines had driven deep into Notre Dame territory late in the game. It was fourth down and inches. They were in danger of losing the game if they did not make the first down.

Most believed the Wolverines would play it safe and run the ball. They instead shocked the sellout crowd at

Explosive Wolverines wide receiver Desmond Howard showed the talent that earned him the Heisman Trophy on this touchdown run in a 31–3 victory over Ohio State in the Big House.

Michigan Stadium. Grbac launched a pass to the corner of the end zone. Howard dove for the ball with his arms fully extended and snagged it with his fingertips just before it hit the ground. Touchdown! The Wolverines won, 24–14.

Howard also created one of the most memorable moments in college football history during the nationally televised showdown against Ohio State in 1991. He sprinted 93 yards on a punt return for a touchdown. He then turned in the end zone and struck the pose of the player on the Heisman Trophy.

It was his way of claiming that he deserved to win the prestigious award. Michigan won that game, 31–3. It was the most lopsided victory over the Buckeyes in forty-five years. Howard indeed became the first Wolverine to win the Heisman Trophy since Tom Harmon in 1940.

STILL WAITING FOR A TITLE

Such greatness from Desmond Howard did not soothe the feelings of Michigan fans still yearning to celebrate a national championship. Many believed Moeller was not the coach who could get that done. He was fired and replaced by assistant Lloyd Carr after back-to-back 8-4 seasons.

Carr was more easygoing than Schembechler or Moeller. But his style of encouraging his players did not translate into greater success in his first two years. The Wolverines had lost four games in four straight seasons. They were becoming an afterthought in the Big Ten and around the country.

Then came 1997. By that time, Moeller had assembled some of the greatest talent in college football. Quarterback Brian Griese led a steady offense that scored at least 20 points every game. Cornerback Charles Woodson earned Big Ten Defensive Player of the Year honors as Michigan yielded just 9.5 points a game to rank first in the nation.

The Wolverines catapulted to number one in the national rankings by clobbering second-ranked Penn State. They clinched an unbeaten regular season with a 20–14 win over Ohio State. Only a Rose Bowl showdown against Washington State stood between the Wolverines and a coveted national championship.

Tackle Jon Jansen wrote the following about his thoughts and those of his teammates in the book *What It Means to Be a Wolverine*: "We hadn't won a Big Ten championship, hadn't been to the Rose Bowl, and we were sick and tired of everyone talking about how, 'Michigan went to four Rose Bowls in a row

A MAN NAMED BRADY

A sophomore quarterback watched from the sideline as Michigan steamrolled to the national championship in 1997. Coach Lloyd Carr did not believe he was good enough to start over Brian Griese. His name was Tom Brady.

Brady started in 1998 and 1999 and emerged as one of the better quarterbacks in college football. He completed 63 percent of his passes for 2,586 yards, 20 touchdowns, and 6 interceptions as a senior. He led Michigan to a 20-5 record in his two years as a starter.

He was not considered an elite NFL prospect. One quarterback after another was selected in the 2000 draft before Brady. He feared that he might be passed over completely. The New England Patriots finally snagged him in the sixth round.

They were not sorry. Brady blossomed into one of the greatest quarterbacks in NFL history. He peaked in 2007, setting a league record with fifty touchdown passes. He guided the Patriots to three Super Bowl titles. It is no wonder that Brady is ticketed for the Pro Football Hall of Fame.

and then the program went down.' We weren't going to be the guys that let the past guys down. A lot of players on our team believed, 'Enough is enough! This is our year, let's go out and do it.'"

FINALLY CROWNED

The Wolverines did go out and do it. The stars shined on New Year's Day in 1998. Griese threw for 251 yards and 3 touchdowns. Wide receiver Taj Streets caught scoring passes of 58 and 53 yards. Linebacker Dhani Jones recorded two sacks on Cougars quarterback Ryan Leaf. Woodson added his eighth interception of the year. He would soon be the first defensive player ever to earn the Heisman Trophy. When the final tick went off the game clock, Michigan owned a 21–16 victory and its first national title since 1948.

It appeared that another undefeated season and national championship was on the horizon in 2006. Michigan and Ohio State prepared for their clash that year unbeaten and ranked 1 and 2 in the nation. Then tragedy struck. Schembechler died of a massive heart attack the day before the epic showdown.

The Wolverines were inspired to win for their fallen legend. But their defense could not stop the Buckeyes, and they lost, 42–39. It was the highest-scoring Ohio State–Michigan game since 1902. Michigan quarterback Chad Henne expressed sadness to Associated Press writer Ralph D. Russo that his team could not beat its archrival in memory of Schembechler. "It was definitely difficult for us," Henne said. "Coach Carr loves him dearly and so do we. . . . It's sad to see him go. We dearly miss him. We tried to fight for him today."

The fight has never gone out of the Wolverines. But they did lose their way after Carr retired in 2007 and

Speedy Michigan quarterback Denard Robinson, one of the most exciting players in college football, sprints for a first down in a 12–10 victory over visiting Michigan State on October 20, 2012.

was replaced by West Virginia coach Rich Rodriguez. The Wolverines plummeted to 3-9 in 2008, their worst record since 1936, and 5-7 in 2009. They had not suffered through successive losing seasons in forty-six years.

They bounced back in 2011 under new coach Brady Hoke and exciting quarterback Denard Robinson. They steamrolled to an 11-2 record that included wins over Ohio State and Virginia Tech in the Sugar Bowl.

The Wolverines were again one of the premier teams in college football. That was nothing new. They had been among the best in the nation since they first set foot on a football field in 1879.

1879: Michigan beats Racine College on May 30 in first football game.

1885–1887: Team wins every game it plays by a combined score of 222–0.

1901: Fielding Yost becomes coach and embarks on era of dominance.

1902: Wolverines win first Rose Bowl game on January 1, beating Stanford, 49–0.

1927: Michigan Stadium opens on October 1.

1933: Wolverines win their second straight national title under Coach Harry Kipke.

1938: Fritz Crisler takes over as coach and enjoys great success.

1940: Tom Harmon wins first Heisman Trophy for Michigan player.

1945: Crisler introduces two-platoon system to college football.

1948: Michigan clobbers USC, 49–0, in Rose Bowl on January 1, but loses out to Notre Dame in national championship vote; new coach Bennie Oosterbaan guides Wolverines to national crown with undefeated season.

1950: Wolverines win at Ohio State, 9–3, in legendary "Snow Bowl" game to clinch fourth straight Big Ten title.

1965: Wolverines conclude 9–1 season with Rose Bowl triumph over Oregon State on January 1.

1969: First-year coach Bo Schembechler guides Wolverines to epic 24–12 upset over Ohio State on November 22.

1972–1974: Michigan embarks on twenty-one-game winning streak, but never plays in bowl game due to Big Ten rules.

1991: Desmond Howard wins second Heisman Trophy in school history.

1997: Defensive back Charles Woodson becomes first defensive player to win Heisman Trophy.

1998: Michigan caps off national championship season on January 1 with 21–16 defeat of Washington State in Rose Bowl; Tom Brady takes over as starting quarterback and later emerges as NFL superstar.

2006: Wolverines fall to Ohio State, 42–39, on November 18 to ruin unbeaten season the day after legendary coach Bo Schembechler dies.

2008: Michigan falls to 3–9 under new coach Rich Rodriguez, its worst season since 1936.

2011: Wolverines bounce back with 11–2 record behind new coach Brady Hoke and star quarterback Denard Robinson.

2012: A 41–14 loss to second-ranked Alabama to open the season ends hope for a national championship; quarterback Denard Robinson totals nearly 2,000 yards rushing and passing combined in the first five games; wins over Illinois and Michigan State place the Wolverines in the top twenty-five in both the Associated Press and *USA Today* college football rankings.

archrival An opponent that brings out great emotion on both sides, often due to its history, tradition, and greatness of programs, such as Michigan against Ohio State.

Big Ten The conference in which Michigan plays.

defensive back A player responsible for covering receivers.

demoralizing Discouraging; causing someone to lose confidence or hope.

halfback An offensive player generally responsible for carrying the ball.

Heisman Trophy An award given annually to the best player in college football that season.

interception A pass caught by the opposing team.

quarterback The most important player on the field— responsible for throwing passes and handing the ball to running backs.

recruiting The act of coaches working to convince top high school athletes to play sports for their college program.

resign To leave a coaching job voluntarily.

Rose Bowl An annual postseason game traditionally including a top team from the Big Ten.

shutout A game in which one team scores zero points.

two-platoon A system in which two separate units of players are used for defense and offense.

upset A game in which the team expected to win does not.

College Football Hall of Fame

111 South Saint Joseph Street

South Bend, IN 46601

(574) 235-9999

Web site: http://www.collegefootball.org

The College Football Hall of Fame boasts information and exhibits about the greatest players and coaches in the history of the sport. Included are such Michigan greats at Tom Harmon and Fielding Yost.

Margaret Dow Towsley Sports Museum

1000 South State

Ann Arbor, MI 48104

(734) 747-2583

More than one hundred years of Michigan football are celebrated at this museum, otherwise known as Schembechler Hall. Included are displays and stories about Michigan athletes, Big Ten titles, and Rose Bowl victories.

Michigan Sports Hall of Fame

P.O. Box 1073

Farmington, MI 48332

(248) 473-0656

Web site: http://www.michigansportshof.org

This online hall of fame and museum features many Michigan football greats. Among the most recent inductees was Lloyd Carr, who coached the Wolverines to the 1997 national title.

Michigan Stadium

1201 South Main Street

Ann Arbor, MI 48104

(734) 647-2583

Web site: http://www.umich.edu

This legendary football stadium is where the Wolverines play their home games. Such future NFL stars as Dan Dierdorf and Tom Brady have performed here.

Pro Football Hall of Fame

2121 George Halas Drive Northwest

Canton, OH 44708

(330) 456-8207

Web site: http://www.profootballhof.com

This hall of fame and museum spotlights the greatest players and moments in the history of the National Football League. Many former Michigan players, including Len Ford and Bennie Friedman, have been inducted there.

WEB SITES

Due to the changing nature of Internet links, Rosen Publishing has developed an online list of Web sites related to the subject of this book. This site is updated regularly. Please use this link to access the list:

http://www.rosenlinks.com/AMWT/MIFB

Boyles, Bob, and Paul Guido. *The USA TODAY College Football Encyclopedia 2010–2011: A Comprehensive Modern Reference to America's Most Colorful Sport, 1953–Present.* New York, NY: Skyhorse Publishing, 2010

Doeden, Matt. *Tom Brady* (Sports Heroes & Legends). Minneapolis, MN: Twenty-First Century Books, 2009.

Editors of Sports Illustrated. *Sports Illustrated: The College Football Book.* New York, NY: Sports Illustrated, 2008.

Jacobs, Greg. *The Everything Kids' Football Book: The All-Time Greats, Legendary Teams, Today's Superstars and Tips on Playing Like a Pro.* Avon, MA: Adams Media, 2008.

Kaufman, Gabriel. *Football in the Big Ten* (Inside College Football). New York, NY: Rosen Publishing, 2007.

Mishler, Todd. *Blood, Sweat and Cheers: Great Football Rivalries of the Big Ten.* Madison, WI: Trails Books, 2007.

Quigley, Brendan Emmett. *Go Michigan! Crossword Puzzle Book: 25 All-New Football Trivia Puzzles.* Kennebunkport, ME: Cider Mill Press, 2008.

Rappoport, Ken. *Michigan Wolverines* (Inside College Football). Edina, MN: ABDO Publishing Company, 2012.

Stewart, Mark. *The Michigan Wolverines* (Team Spirit). Chicago, IL: Norwood House Press, 2009.

Thomaselli, Rich. *I Love Michigan/I Hate Ohio State.* Chicago, IL: Triumph Books, 2011.

Turner, Michelle L. *The Rose Bowl: Images of America.* Mount Pleasant, SC: Arcadia Publishing, 2010.

Yuen, Kevin. *The 10 Most Intense College Football Rivalries.* New York, NY: Children's Press/Franklin Watts, 2008.

Allen, Kevin, Nate Brown, and Art Regner. *What It Means to Be a Wolverine.* Chicago, IL: Triumph Books, 2005.

Athlon Sports. *Game Day: Michigan Football.* Chicago, IL: Triumph Books, 2006.

Bentley Historical Library. "University of Michigan Athletics History." Retrieved September 30, 2012 (http://www .bentley.umich.edu/athdept/olymp2/ol1936.htm).

Cantor, George. *Michigan Football: Yesterday and Today.* Lincolnwood, IL: West Side Publishing, 2008.

Dunn, Mike. "Postscript: Wolverines Played in 1901 Rose Bowl, Beating Stanford." *Petoskey News*, December 23, 2003. Retrieved September 18, 2012 (http://articles.petoskeynews .com/2003-12-22/wolverine-fans_24068450).

Falk, Jim. *If These Walls Could Talk: Michigan Football Stories from the Big House.* Chicago, IL: Triumph Books, 2010.

Manus, Willard. "Passing Recognition." University of Michigan News Service, Fall 2004. Retrieved September 18, 2012 (http://michigantoday.umich.edu/04/Fall04/story.html ?passing).

Maxwell, Fredrick Alan. "The Late Great 98: Tom Harmon on the Field and at War." *Michigan Today,* September 17, 2008. Retrieved September 30, 2012 (http://michigantoday. umich.edu/2008/09/harmon.php).

Russo, Ralph D. "No. 1 Ohio State 42, No. 2 Michigan 39." Yahoo! Sports, November 18, 2006. Retrieved October 10, 2012 (http://rivals.yahoo.com/ncaa/football/recap?gid=20061 1180033).

INDEX

ABOUT THE AUTHOR

Marty Gitlin is an educational book writer and sportswriter based in Cleveland, Ohio. He has had more than seventy books published in the realms of sports, history, social studies, and entertainment. He has also written biographies about notable people in all walks of life. Included among his books are histories of the Ohio State and the University of Florida football programs. Gitlin has written many books about college and professional sports. He also covers the NFL Cleveland Browns for CBSSports.com. During his twenty years as a newspaper sportswriter, he won more than forty-five awards, including first-place general excellence from Associated Press. He lives in Ohio with his wife and three children.

PHOTO CREDITS

Cover, p. 1 Jamie Sabau/Getty Images; back cover (goal post) David Lee/Shutterstock.com; p. 4 Diamond Images/Getty Images; p. 5 Andrew Horne/Wikipedia.org/Michigan Stadium 2011.jpg/CC BY-SA 3.0; pp. 7, 17, 24, 27, 29 © AP Images; pp. 9, 10, 13, 14, 20, 31 Bentley Image Bank, Bentley Historical Library, University of Michigan; pp. 16, 38 Leon Halip/Getty Images; p. 22 The Ohio State University Archives; p. 34 Chris Covatta/Getty Images; multiple interior page borders and boxed text backgrounds (football) Nickola_Che/Shutterstock .com; pp. 6, 12, 19, 26, 33 (helmet) from a photo by Al Messerschmidt/Getty Images; back cover and multiple interior pages background (abstract pattern) © iStockphoto .com/Che McPherson.

Designer: Brian Garvey; Editor: Kathy Kuhtz Campbell; Photo Researcher: Amy Feinberg